Don't Drop Me, God

Don't Drop Me, God

LUCY BELL SELLERS

P O E M S

NYOKA PRESS
PHILADELPHIA

To my husband Peter, and our four children
Tim, Therese, Wanja, and Lucy Bell

Contents

POEMS for FAMILY

EMBU DISTRICT, KENYA 1961

MORE POEMS

FOR FUN

EARLY

Trust

The waves are big today, but my small son,
Clinging with his toes like any monkey child,
Hangs for dear life upon my back and laughs
To find the sea so wild.

He fears the sea, all right, knows that it can
Batter you down until you're choking on the beach
With half the seashore up your pants and in your eyes,
And you too weak to scramble out of reach.

And then there are the crabs,
But they're no matter now,
And neither are the waves for all my son could care,
High warm and handsome on my back,
Such is his trust in me, when I am there.
Why I should have this trust, God only knows.
Don't drop me, God.
The waves are big.
The crabs nibble at my toes.

On Listening to a Scholarly Lecture in Spring

He speaks, my sweet, of Merovingian kings,
Which he, since but a youngster here, has tracked
Around the labyrinth of doubtful truths
In that dark wood of controversial fact.

What are his kings to me that I should sit
And copy down the dates he thinks they died
When I smell lilacs blooming in the yard
And all Spring's robins call me to your side?

But what were they to him?
When he smelled lilacs, why did he not stray
Unless some vision which he thought he saw
Seemed sweet and bright and beautiful as they?

Can I presume to call his vision false,
A scholar's fantasy that I need not pursue?
I might, if I could manage to forget
Those kings heard robins too,
And having heard them, died.

So I will sit and struggle toward that sun
That can turn kings, springs and you and me to one.

Clowns

I realize now it never wasn't there.
We walked so high and barefoot on the buoyant moss.
The sun dazzled our eyes.
Our ears were filled with waterfalls and white throats' cries,
And we could smell the summer in each breath.

But when I saw it, I was not afraid.
You held my hand, staying my fear of falling at your touch.
Our paths skirted the air.
Like clowns, we balanced by the chasms where
The shadowed valley threatened every step.

I don't know how I fell,
But suddenly I was alone in somewhere bare and grey.
My hands trembled with cold.
You waved above me, but my voice went old,
And though I called, you couldn't understand.

I never thought I'd walk the heights again,
But here we are, balancing once more.
The rocks glitter below,
So take my hand, and quickly let us go
And dare to dance defiance while we may.

Gold

Within the moments of my love,
I walk in gold and giving grain
Which, by the fullness of its ears,
Returns the softness of the rain.

FORMS

Babies

Eve and Adam gloried in Cain's birth
And greeted his arrival with such joy,
As if he were the only child on earth,
Their first, unique and perfect little boy.
When Abel came, it was the same again.
Another miracle! Another life!
They had no foresight of the moment when
Their world would shatter in fraternal strife.
The ill that lies ahead is out of sight,
But if experience has proved it true,
Why do we have this instinct of delight
At every prospect of a life's that's new?
In reason, such rejoicing 's out of place,
But reason doesn't propagate the race.

A Tomboy Grows Older

If all your growing years, you'd tagged along,
And tried, incessantly, to be a guy
And ached to show that you were just as strong
As your big brothers, if they'd let you try.
Then, when adult, you'd never be the same.
You wouldn't want to sit back and observe,
But nurse a desp'rate need to join each game
To prove your speed, your spirit and your nerve.
So now, how odd, to watch the game apart,
And, even odder, not to mind at all
At merely watching all that brawn and breath.
"Let youth," I think, "delight in skill and heart,
I'd spoil their fun, if I should have a fall."
Now is that wisdom, or a step towards death?

The Ballad of Mr. Mc Gregor

My lettuce was my heart's desire,
My lettuce was my pride.
My lettuce was the envy of
The country far and wide.

One day I viewed my lettuce,
And found to my dismay,
That some unholy villain
Had nibbled it away,

Had nibbled it to nothing
And stripped it to the root
And like our sinful ancestor
Had chomped forbidden fruit.

I harbored my suspicions,
But looked around for clues
And saw, among the carnage,
Young Peter Rabbit's shoes.

With long hoe at the ready,
I went on the attack.
"As sure as I'm McGregor,
I'm going to pay you back!"

"I'm going to pay you back!" said I,
"I'll bake you in a pie!
You'll leave my lettuces alone
 Or know the reason why."

I chased him through the cabbages,
I chased him round the hay,
Then, scrounging underneath a gate,
That rabbit got away.

This sissy little jacket
Is all he left, alack,
But sure as I'm McGregor,
I'm going to pay him back.

The Ballad of the
Stafford St. Spruce

"Too close to the house."
"Casts too much shade."
"Probably ready to fall."
For fifty years, they've been after my tree,
And I have resisted them all.

Still who can resist
The hand of fate
Or foil what the gods decree,
When they conjure a rogue of a terrible storm
To threaten my beautiful tree?

The branches whipped wildly,
The trunk was besieged.
Heroic, the tree held fast.
Until, in the end, a toehold gave,
And the tree tipped over at last.

The tree tipped over,
But not so far
That the house was damaged a whit.
In halting disaster a foot from the roof,
Was the brave tree doing its bit?

Was I ungrateful?
Had I a choice?
It was clear that the tree must go,
So why, when arranging to take my friend down,
Did I feel so guilty and low?

In fitting grandeur,
The tree left home
With cranes that reached to the sky
And an army of arborists on the alert
To ready the novice to fly.

Over the roofs,
The tree took flight
Happy as never before,
Rhythmically flapping its feathery wings,
Free as an angel to soar.
Don't let it be said
The tale is told.
The point of it's still to be.
The tree I protected for fifty years
Went down while protecting me.

Fine

When asked, I always answer, "Fine."
They hear it with relief.
It's hard to comfort such a loss as mine.

They take my reassurance as a sign
That I have mastered grief.
When asked, I always answer, "Fine."

I never let them know how I confine
My sadness, hidden like a thief.
It's hard to comfort such a loss as mine.

Alone, there isn't need to hold the line
Against the outbursts, violent but brief.
When asked, I always answer "Fine."

Set off by nothing, toothpaste, pictures, wine,
The trigger's triviality belies belief.
It's hard to comfort such a grief as mine.

I've not been here before, I can't divine
The tree's importance by the leaf.
When asked, I always answer "Fine."
It's hard to comfort such a loss as mine.

Sand Castles

The tide's devouring the castled sand.
The unsuspecting children are asleep.
How can they know destruction is at hand?

The sleeping children do not understand,
So have no fears for sandy moat or keep.
The tide's devouring the castled sand.

Too trusting in the permanence of land,
They do not dream the water gets so deep.
How can they know destruction is at hand?

Should we have put a stop to what they planned,
Because we'd witnessed how the sea could leap?
The tide's devouring the castled sand.

We held our peace while spades and pails were manned,
Too cowardly, by far, to make a peep.
When should they know destruction is at hand?

We, too, have lost our careful castles and
Have suffered from the sea's determined creep.
The tide's devouring the castled sand.
We know, we know destruction is at hand.

PLANTS,
ANIMALS,
and
SEASONS

To a Loon at Sunrise

It seems, old Loon, on this whole lake
There's just the two of us awake.
Well I have had an idle line,
Has your luck been as bad as mine?
If so, you'll have to go unfed,
While I'll fall back on toast instead,
Which goes to show, as I can see,
How different you are from me.
But I have seen you dive from sight
And heard the wailing of your call,
So fellow fisher, black and white,
Are we not kinsmen after all?

Night Loon

Cry, Loon, cry.
We share the night,
And your lone wailing over an empty lake
Speaks for us all.

On Seeing a Bluebird

A bluebird! emblem of delight!
But was I quite irrevocably sure?
The colors were admittedly obscure,
And too much hoping undermines the sight.

I see him! There he is again!
I'll follow, then,
To seek a certain view.
He lights, I wait, at last, the telling blue.

Joy will return,
Though only God knows when.

The Snowmen

Look! The snowmen have come out.
They stand in frozen expectation on the lawn
As if awaiting the photographer.
Their clothing contradicts their formal pose.
Their rakish hats and cheerful scarves
Are worn for neither modesty nor warmth
But purely for the fun.
How fine the snowmen are!
How brave, assured of certain melting,
To stand and watch the world
With eager, coal black eyes.

Shoveling the Walk
for the Elderly

I've seen them navigate the snowy walks
With all the concentration of a mountaineer
Bent on his preservation by an icy edge.
Who wouldn't want to spare them that?
So with a will, I shovel out a way.
But when the sidewalk's clean,
The lovely snow, fluffy and pristine,
Has turned, by my own efforts,
Ugly, packed, and grey.

Robins in Winter

The robins have come back.
Mistakenly, they're singing that it's spring.
It's obvious that something is amiss.
But make the most of it
And let them sing.

First Robin

Good old robin,
Hopping fatly on my faulty lawn
And hauling worms from my unlikely mud.
A single robin may not make a Spring,
But you sure make my garden.

Reprieved

I knew the measure of the spring I'd miss.
My six bright tulips blooming unextolled,
My daffodils, abandoned and bereft,
My iris squandering their velvet gold.
I mourned each primrose that would bloom and pass,
The tender colors of the waking wood,
The peonies, the lilacs, and the grass,
And tried to think my travel plans were good.
I left it all prepared to pay the cost,
And came away resigned to everything.
But once arrived, I found what I had lost:
Tulips, lilacs, daffodils—my spring!

Lost Blooming

The multiflora roses came and went without me there.
I missed the lilacs too.
By Housman's reckoning my time is up.
How shall I compensate for my great loss?

Spring Delight

It's Spring, so everyone is out,
The bees in their flowers,
The squirrels in their trees,
The neighbors on their clever phones.
"Hello," they say to me as I walk by.
"Hello," they say into their clever phones.
"Hello! Hello! Hello!"
They're just that pleased they're still alive.

Spring

Shoots are shooting!
Crows are crowing!
Streams are streaming!
Snows aren't snowing!
As for me, I'm going, going,
Going out to greet the Spring!

My Garden

For *House and Garden,* my garden wouldn't rate.
A feast of ordered bounty it is not.
No editor would waste one color plate
On such a ragged and unpolished plot.

No trophy garden, though, could please me more
Than this, my little patch of soil and weeds,
Whose spotty produce, limited in store,
Has nonetheless been grown from my own seeds.

When disconnection makes me not to thrive,
My garden gives me somewhere I can go
To feel some purpose, or, at least, alive
And that is why I love my garden so.

The Garden Porcupine

A porcupine, appearing to reside
In our late garden, threatens to remain.
 My last few beets are nothing but a stain
On his white teeth. Will he abide
To finish up the chard with prickled joy?
Oh, let him eat the tidbits he has found.
He's more than welcome to my fallow ground.
What, after all, is left he could destroy?

Epitaph for a Garden

Here lie hopes of garden glory
Dashed by mean, marauding deer.
Pilgrim pause and think with pity
Of the dreams that perished here.

Amtrak Naturalist

Skyline drawing ever nearer
Towards New York my Amtrak hurtles,
If I'm lucky, out the window,
I'll see herons, ducks, and turtles.

Ducks in the Serpentine

No barbarian, I honor what I ought,
Frequent the Tate, the Abbey and St Paul's,
Admire what I should, as I've been taught,
And quickly fall in line when culture calls.
My London trip? What did I like the best
Among the city's rich historic mix?
Why rowing on the Serpentine
And seeing all the fluffy little chicks.

Immortality I

The reddish radiance
Of every maple bough
Says life is deathless.
But how? But how?

Immortality II

Seven goslings,
Newly hatched at dawn,
Fuzzy assurance
That life goes on.

Bath with a Beetle

Small for a bomber,
Big for a bug.
A beetle buzzes me
In my bath,
Banks around for a fresh assault and crashes.
Timidly, I leave my bath to reconnoiter
And find my enemy belly up, his little legs waving
    in the air.
"Good," I think, and go to bed.

Come the morning, I am miserable with shame.
To leave a fellow creature,
Even a belligerent beetle,
Writhing on the floor for one whole night!
Crushed with remorse, I go to gather the remains.
But no, no remains at all, but a beetle unhurt,
    right side up
And ready to go.
This time, wary still, I wrap him in a wash rag,
    take him to the door
And let him go. It's seldom you get a second chance.

The Tree

With love and living springs the tree was nourished,
And everyone admired how it flourished,
Until, one day, for no apparent reason,
 Quite independently of storm or season,
The lush leaves flew, as one, into the air
And left the stripped tree desolate and bare.

Green

Green, green, green,
And all the sparrows singing in the sun.
Oh God, let me be green again
And sing.

The Pond

We dug a pond
 Or rather had one dug.
A scoop, a truck,
A place to put the muck.
Easy.

And then the wait.

First came the amorous Toads
Double decked in shameless copulation.

Then their ugly ropes of eggs
Twisted around and around like tangled wire.

The ropes gave way to zillions of black and tiny tadpoles
Who, massed together, blackened the water's edge.

The frogs came next, one by one, parentless
But known by the pitch of every satisfying plop.

Afterward, the snakes, three skinny ones
And a big fat one who dove headfirst into the water
    out of a tree.

Then the turtles. Three painted turtles and one little
    snapping turtle
Who terrorized the tadpoles.

Finally, one female wood duck, who flew away.

What ducks will stay?
What surprising life will settle in,
Drawn by the water of our pond?

POEMS
for
FAMILY

Town and Boma

False fronts flat in the noonday heat
Thrust, rectangular, to the skies
Along both sides of a wide brown street,
Which might, if weren't "Madhubais,"
The "Kaids" and "Bhikus" over the door,
Be running through any Wyoming town
With brown men lounging around the stores
And dusty cattle ambling down.
Lazily down on the road below,
White collared ayahs, dressed in blue,
Push white charges beneath the trees.
Sons of police and daughters, too,
Of Barclay's bank and the new D.C.
Mackley, Parfitt and Watson-Jones,
Goldsworthy, Baker and Sutton and Morse,
Neat black letters on neat white signs
Look across at the Embu course.

The Mountain

With humility and awe,
Even the Christian lifts his eyes
Whenever the home of the pagan gods
Displays his grandeur against the skies.
And during the days of the hanging mist,
Which turns the palace to flat, grey plain,
Even the Christian tries and tries
To penetrate to the peaks again.
Strange expanses of frozen snows,
Desolate moorland and vast bamboo,
Elephants, leopards and buffaloes
Fade to innocent white and blue.
But neither distance nor mist obscures
From the minds of men what they know is there.
Christian and pagan stop alike,
Turn to the mountain and stand and stare.

Down Murinduko Way

Fold back the canvas! Brace your legs!
Give with the jolts without dismay!
Don't turn back from the sisal track,
We're heading down Murinduko way!

Crash through the bushes! Over the grass!
Don't let the lookout fall asleep!
Four wheels four will help no more
When you're stuck in a burrow three feet deep.

Kingfishers flash, hornbills skulk,
While impalas' black tipped ears
Twitch and pass in the high brown grass
In quick response to the lone buck's fears.

Back to the road and faster! Faster!
Roll down the mountain onto the plain
Where burning air and windless glare
Make scrub thorns shiver, as if in pain.

Count the impala by the herd,
Watch them leaping to cross ahead,
Hartebeests, too, go running through,
Awkward brown among graceful red.

Now baboons come hurtling over.
Black forms flying on burnt out black
Fade from sight in the midst of flight
As we enter a new and darker track.

Hundreds of silent footprints tell
Of myriad beasts in the thick, dead brush.
Now no sound on trampled ground,
Or even a bird disturbs the hush.

Listen ahead, as sound returns
In rushing water and jungle cry,
Flung to the breeze from jungle trees
Hung with orchids, blooming high.

Left hand river and right-hand stream
Meet in the middle and round the bend.
Foot prints stop at the bank's sharp drop,
And the water begins at the long road's end.

The Plain

Vast dry ocean to rest the eyes on,
Stretching out to the far horizon,
With waves of yellow and purple and red,
Or a great, still basin of blue, instead.

Kangaru School

School Cert, football, prep and rhumbas,
Turn Ngigis to Mujumbas.

With Mary in Central Park

Nobody's Central Park is quite the same.
For one, it's children on the granite slide,
It's yellow daffodils for someone else,
For others, it's a place to blade or ride.
For him, it's birding in the ramble,
For her, it's going to the children's zoo.
He likes the statue of the noble dog,
She likes a special bench when day is through.
My Central Park's like no one else's;
It's looking for you, when my biking's done
And suddenly seeing, way in the distance,
You coming toward me at an easy run.

Squid Cove

Why should blue heron's make me think of you?
They're long in neck and legs, as you are not,
And 'though you share a common dignity,
That's not the reason that I think, "Aunt Marge,"
When I've the luck to spot one overhead
Or standing, handsome, at the water's edge.

Of course, the link's Squid Cove,
That happy place for herons and for you,
The place where you and they,
Among the loons, seals, rocks and tides
Are always home.

When species share a habitat with grace,
They must be kin.

On Watching Therese Cry

So now she cries
And I, bewildered, but undone
Stand dumbly by my daughter's crumpled heart
A quarter century apart.

So she, at crying of my own,
Will some day stand,
In equal pain, when grown,
And try, in equal unbelief,
To puzzle out my secret grief.

So dear Therese, if I don't understand,
I love you still,
And offer you my hand.

On Finding a Shark's Tooth in the Wash

When all the drawers were emptied down once more,
To levels of the stained, ill-fitting and the torn,
I went to face the laundry where it lay
Neglected in my room, unsorted and unworn.

I hadn't chased the chaos very far
(A sock for him, a shirt for her, a dress for me,)
When suddenly among the piles appeared
A black and shiny shark's tooth from the sea.

I placed it my palm and saw again
The wild gulf nibbling the strand,
The fierce gulls jostling for bread,
The bright coquinas captured in my hand.

Because of sharks, I guess, I thought about the Shark,
That dark and secret mangrove crowded stream,
Where alligators float across the top,
And disappear, as silent as a dream.

And then I firmly pocketed my prize
And went about my sorting job once more.
(A sock for him, a shirt for her, a dress for me.)
The same old thing, but different from before,

Our laundry sorting lives are saved, in part,
By sharp toothed shiny treasures of the heart.

LOSS

1. The Choice

Too important to be wearing white,
Our doctor stands before us at his ease.
We sit, uneasily, and wait to hear our fate
Which is:
Battle the cancer, no holds barred
Or go for quality of life.
"The choice is yours," the doctor says.
"You have to find the balance for yourselves"
How can he think we have the light to choose
When he, himself, is in the dark?

2 . Good Luck

Usually, they take their seats in twos,
And usually, you can't discern who's sick.
When called, they go within.
Then they emerge, put on their coats and disappear.
You never see the same pair twice. You never speak.
But once or twice, stuck outside some treatment room,
The last to leave,
The other wife will turn to you and say,
"Good luck."
"The same to you," you say, and turn away.

3 . Maine

Did Maine go away when we did?
Is it still there?

4. Calling Chris

At nine o'clock, you ask to talk to Chris.
"It's never been so bad," you say,
"He had a special pet scan yesterday," you say.
"He's due for radiation soon," you say
They tell you Chris will call you back.
So then you wait and wait and wait.
At four o'clock, the call comes through.
You get it on the second ring.
You get a recording with a number to call.
You call it.
The number doesn't answer.
You run eight and a half blocks to the doctor's office.
"I want to talk to Chris," you say.
They tell you she is seeing patients.
"I'll wait," you say.
And then you wait and wait and wait and wait.
Five after five, Chris appears,
Not the ogre you expected,
But a pretty young woman, who, except for the white coat,
Could be your granddaughter.
And she is so charming and so forthcoming
That you are mollified.
Until the next time that you want to talk to Chris.

5. Two Medicine Poems

My dearest love is sick.
I see it in his face,
His pace,
His getting up and in his lying down.
I see it on his bedside table.
So many pills.

(After Ophelia)
There's prednizone.
That's for adrenaline,
Pray you, love, remember.
That's baby aspirin for the heart
And Mirilax for regularity.
There's Cipro for infections,
And Tylenol to stop the pain.
O' Sundays there is Oxycodone.
Hey nonny, nonny, nonny hey nonny.
We must be patient.
I hope all will be well.

6. Bright Spots

An Australian ketch,
Bucking the East River tide
And flaunting the Southern Cross
Has saved my day,
Together with the market man
Who smiled at me, and said,
"Where have you BEEN?"

7. Hello Out There

Email, texting,
Beggarman, thief.
Cell phone, land line,
Merchant chief.
White to white and black to black.
Give me my connection back.
Merchant, beggarman,
I don't care.
Maybe, there's some thief out there
Who, for a shiny cherry stone,
Would come to make me less alone.

8. Painting in the Garden

Another garden scene?
Why not?
What better way to pass the time
Than in the vain attempt
To catch a light
Forever out of reach?

Monet, with all those waterlilies
Was he, too, hoping to redeem the time
Whose hours too swiftly
Didn't fly.

9. Luckier than Lear

Luckier than Lear
Your growing old is blessed
With three Cordelias.

Dark

At the start, you're altogether in the dark.
The first glimmers aren't so bad,
Your friend's father or your grandfather who lives in Ohio.
Enlightenment comes fast,
Your college roommate or your Dad,
And then the list becomes so long you have to mark
   down "died" in your address book.
You don't expect this blinding light of loss
That sends you creeping back into the dark.

What Are We?

Don't call us "The Bereaved,"
A phrase for funeral homes
Or Hallmark cards.

What are we then?

Sailors, stripped of charts and compass.
Walkers, wet and spent and wanting home.
Acrobats who've lost their nerve.

Refugees
Explorers
Pioneers

Recent settlers in a lonely land.

Fine

Fine.
They ask me "how are you?"
And I say "fine."
They mean, "Are you OK now you're alone?"
I still say, "fine."
I eat and sleep, garden, ride my bike and take delight in
    family and friends.
Fine.
Recently, I saw a man in a blue shirt and khaki pants.
Just for a second, I thought it was Peter.
Of course it wasn't.
Fine.

The Picture

Still and silent in your leather frame,
You smile at me with your lovely smile.
As I smile back, something shifts inside me,
A little earthquake along a major fault.
I think I still can see you in the flesh,
But I'm not sure.

Careless Ways

My love indulged my careless ways.
With care enough for two,
He saved me from improvidence
So that I never missed a train or lost my way.
For this I gave him grief instead of gratitude.

"Why do we have to leave the house so early?"
"Can't you stop looking at the map?"

Now I'm alone
And you should see me watch the clock and scan the map,
Except I'm always lost.

Memories

When you were here, our past was memories no less
    than it is now.
"Do you remember?" was a pleasant game.
But when you died, those memories grew teeth to
    snap and bite
Whenever I came close.
Are they so sad at losing half their audience,
    they take it out on me?
Who knows?
I know they've turned against me
And make me cry.

"You have your memories," they like to say.
I answer, "Yes."

Socks

They go inside as neatly paired as Noah's animals.
All's well at first, but something goes amiss.
Those happy couples start to lose their mates.
Why?
No one knows.
A laundry flood?
A troll beneath the bed?
A mystery.
But every day, another partner's gone
Till all that's left is lonely widows in the dark.
I wonder how they fare.
Do they make friends?

Cruising

I'd thought my trip was danger free
Our boat was sturdy, sound of hull and mast.
I gloried in each passage and each port
Snatched from the past.

Pain lurks in the particulars,
There's where we walked, we anchored over there,
And there and there and there…

The tides of memory are treacherous,
They raise you up,
But at the ebb,
They bare the hidden ledge
You didn't know was there.
And then you drown.

Do Not Go Gentle 1

"Rage, rage against the dying of the light!"
But is that right?
Rage can't prolong the light by one small spark.
Better, maybe, to embrace the dark,
Accepting all her gifts
Of gratitude and grace.
To face the sunset's splendor or the sun's eclipse.
The eyes need aid, which rage rejects,
So cannot see the skies.
The gentle traveler sits still among his friends
Sharing the sunset while the colors fade.

Do Not Go Gentle 2

Dark begins at Dawn.
Noon's only a diversion from the truth.
The dying starts at birth.
Worth is reckoned by how fierce the fight
To wrestle trophies from the teeth of time.
Acquiescence is the coward's part.
Resist! Resist!
And when they douse the lights to speed the night,
Rage, rage against the dying of the light.

Eighty-Five

Eighty-five.
A ripe old age.
But ripe enough, even then, for danger,
With the stems softening and the fruit ready to fall,
Falling,
Fallen.

Eighty-five.
A ripe old age.
Now the fruits are falling fast,
But still I grieve for the one that fell the first,
So long ago.

Cicada

Grief never dies.
Cicada-like, it burrows deep,
Then in its own good time, it resurrects and flies
On veined, transparent wings.

HAMLET

POEMS

A Lawyer, 32

The shocks that flesh is heir to end in death,
Of evils ultimate, pervasive and complete,
The last corruption of the labored breath,
The final unassailable defeat.

Hamlet, being ready, saw it whole,
Not death alone, but all that death implies,
From lurking serpents in the inmost soul
To public treasons, homicides and lies.

I envy Hamlet, that he found the grace
To brave existence with a steady eye.
When it confronts me, I avert my face,
Ashamed to live, but too afraid to die.

A School Girl, 16

Poor Ophelia, stuck at court,
Phony games, but little sport.
Nothing doing, nothing going,
Where's the fun in closet sewing?
Prying father, prying brother,
One suspicious as the other,
Both such spoilers. Is it odd
Hamlet seemed a gift from God?
Then they trashed his love, as well,
Leaving you alone in hell.
Poor Ophelia, were I you,
I'd be in the river, too.

A Bishop, 63

For more than murder, Claudius was damned.
Remember Lucifer and why he fell.
Of all the sins with which our souls are crammed
There's none like pride to plummet us to hell.
You cannot have your cake and eat it, too,
To have it all belongs to God, alone,
But that's what Claudius presumed to do
In aiming at salvation, queen and throne.
The ways of Claudius are ways I know.
I've never murdered, but we'll meet below.

A Widow, 51

When Harry died, I thought that I'd die too
(Except you don't).
What pulled me through was Harry's brother, Tom.
He looked like Harry and was very kind.
It's only men who harp on lust, lust, lust.
What do they know of sleeping coldly in an empty bed
And living on your own?
I feel for Gertrude, hoping it might work,
That Hamlet, chiefest courtier and son
Could grow to look on Denmark as a friend,
Return to reason and his winning ways
And take Ophelia for his loving wife.
That isn't how it went.

When Harry died, young Harry left the funeral
    straight for school.
If only Hamlet could have done the same,
But no, he had to stay and dig for truth, no matter what,
And the result? The end of Gertrude.
You can't be shown your life's a sham,
Your loved ones, murderers,
Your whole existence rotten to the core,
Your son ashamed to be your son,
And still go on.
I feel for Gertrude.
Death by poison is a fearful thing.

A Retired Business Man, 71

My daughter's daughter took Ophelia's part
In her school's *Hamlet*, which I went to see.
It had, perhaps, more energy than art,
But it's a play that always speaks to me.

Polonius, to my intense surprise
Was not the villain I'd perceived before.
He'd managed, with the years, to metamorphosize
Into an ordinary, well intentioned bore.

Of course, his spying methods were extreme,
But weren't his motives poorly understood?
He did his duty by his chosen team,
And *thought* he'd acted for his children's good.

And yet, for all those deaths he shared the blame,
Though he observed conventions to the letter.
I'm frightened that, at heart, I'm much the same
And haven't in the end, done any better.

To set the world aright was once my pride,
But now, instead, I do as I am told.
I'm glad he never knew his children died.
Polonius! Good God! I must be getting old.

A Minor Politician, 47

I dream of Wittenberg, of Hamlet and Horatio
    fencing for fun
And after, meeting Rosencrantz and Guildenstern
(Weren't they there too?)
To drink and talk philosophy.
For Rosencrantz and Guildenstern, those days were best
(Like college days for me.)
Then they had friends, ideas and dreams of being good.
At Wittenberg, they hadn't yet betrayed a trust,
Mangled the truth, or even known they could.
Which makes them lucky to have died so young.
I dream of Wittenberg,
Where Rosencrantz and Guildenstern,
Forever students, get a second chance.

MORE

POEMS

For Adele Arden, Our Neighbor

Already, when we came, the signs were nailed in place:
Hillman, Delsing, Arden, Saylor,
So from the start, they figured in our scene.
We never thought that they'd be growing frailer.

But after forty years, we might have known
That, sure as fate, their ranks were sure to shrink.
The dogs were first, but after that,
The pool of neighbor men began to sink.

Sam Hillman died the first,
Then Mr. Arden (can't recall his name)
Then David Delsing died, and then some wives,
Ingrid, Reni and Elaine. It was a shame.

But now Adele, I wonder at myself
To mourn her passing with such loud "alas."
Our interactions centered on the drive
When someone backed to let the other pass.

You ought to earn the right to feel so sad.
What impure motives gave my sorrow breath?
Perhaps I grudged diminishing my world,
Or sensed, in hers, my own impending death.

I couldn't say, but when I heard she'd died,
Against all reason, I sat down and cried.

The Lake and the Light

The lake's the playground of the light.
Sun and moon share it between them, half and half,
Agreed on long ago.
Both sun and moon play the old-time games,
Dazzle the Lake and Chase the Waves.
But more than that, they have their special tricks.
Only the moon can silver the fierce, unruly waves to set
    the lake alive with leaping fire.
And only the sun can still each ripple with a magic spell
    and turn the lake to liquid gold.
The lake's not jealous of the sun and moon. They've
    been friends forever.
She likes their tricks, and rightly takes some credit
    for herself.
Besides, she knows they make her beautiful.

Mama

My boat's the Mama,
Named for me
By me.
My first and only boat,
Barely afloat when I earned ownership
By paint, patches and a name.
A young woman and an old boat.
But over time, I've evened up the years,
So now what people see
Is two old mamas
Rowing gently down the lake.

Partire è un Po Morire
(To Leave Is to Die a Little)

I am dying a little.
Goodbye to lake, loons, and milky way.
Good bye to summer.
I'm off to another season's pleasures
Left with equal sadness half a year ago.
Two deaths in a single year.
The wages of a double life.

End of Summer

The end of summer brings the usual dread.
It means that I must leave.
No loons calling as I lie in bed.
No still lake lightening at dawn.
No salt fog streaking from the sea.
No dark sky showing off the stars.
No seals, no porpoises, no boats.
How can I bear it?
I can, and bear it every year.
For there are some I cannot live without,
Even in a lakeless land.

Noah

Did Noah navigate,
Charts spread about him,
Heaving the lead on deck,
In dripping oilskins, scanning for stars?
Or did he stroll the bobbing ark
Beneath a striped umbrella,
Scratching the elephants' ears
And looking for the rainbow?

When the Fog Comes
in from the Sea

The children are making their castles of sand.
The parents are watching them play,
And everything's peaceful and safe and serene
At the beach on a beautiful day.

But then something shifts. The mother gets chilled.
The children fight over the keep.
The father grows angry as things fall apart,
For the fog is beginning to creep.

The children abandon their buckets and pails.
The parents make ready to flee.
The dampness of fear's seeping into their bones
When the fog comes in from the sea.

They sense the surge of the ship running blind
Toward the reefs that are certain to be,
And they breathe the breath of the sailors drowned
When the fog comes in from the sea.

You can sit in the sun when the weather's fine
And feel independent and free.
But you'll breathe the breath of the sailors drowned
When the fog comes in from the sea.

For Peggy

You did love heights, so I, who feared them
Followed you onto Brooklyn roofs
And mountain tops in Maine
To see you in your element of edges and of air.
Now you are dead, and I, though still afraid,
Nevertheless seek out the heights alone
To huddle by the drop,
Remembering you.

Ireland

Not surprisingly, it's green,
But green beyond belief,
A God created foil for castles, crosses
And for grey stone walls.
An Irish miracle
Like Patrick
And the lack of snakes.

On Taking Three Children to the Airport after Christmas

Three times today, I've travelled down this strip
To take another of my children hence.
More sensible, by far, to make a single trip,
But recently, I've been unsound on sense
And conjured visions of domestic bliss
As anyone of reason would eschew
As unrealistic in a world like this,
Where saints and angels commonly are few.

So it is foolishness, or even greed,
To look upon our Christmas with complaints.
We had our share of merriment, indeed,
Did I expect communion of the saints?
I guess I did and still expect it here,
Deciphering "Departures" one last time.
"Which airline are you flying out on, dear?"
Could lead, conceivably to the sublime,
But doesn't much.

A miracle's a gift
That happens only by God's holy grace.
For the presumptuous, the punishment is swift,
The lonely, disappointed drive in this bleak place.

The Turtle Rebuffed

"That's obvious," he said, so she drew back
And eyed him sadly from her painted shell.
However dull, it was a turtle's thought.
A fellow turtle might, for love, have listened well.

Eve's Granddaughter Consoles Her for the Loss of Eden

Eva: Grandma, don't be sad.
It's lovely here and now
And nicer far than that old garden.

Eve: I long for the long, cool dawns,
The robins singing in the gentle dark,
The smell of lilacs
And of flowers still unnamed,
The daily miracle of light.

Eva: But we have robins, too
And dawn each day.

Eve: Not just the dawning, the days, as well.
No decisions and no regrets.
We saw what we should do,
And doing was delight.
We heard the music,
And our steps were sure.

Eva: Aha! "Should do! "
It's what I thought.
You hadn't any choice.

Eve: But choosing didn't enter in.

Eva: How could it not?

Eve: Like breathing.
You don't choose to breathe.

Eva: There! You've admitted it!

Eve: Well then, we always chose,
We just chose right.
Imagine melodies so sweet…

Eva: I still don't get it, and I never will.
Grandma, cheer up.

Eve: But don't you understand?
The snake and I were friends!

It

I see its heels slipping around the corner.
I hear it whispering, but miss the words.
It brushes against my leg.
It's like a bird that tempts discovery
But won't be found.
It drives me wild!
If I could just be quicker at the corner,
Or catch the words, or spot the bird,
I'd get to join the dance.
And I'd know how.

Corinthians I:13 Envy

"Charity suffereth long and is kind; charity envieth not;
    charity vaunteth not itself; is not puffed up…
    rejoices not in iniquity."

I don't vaunt very much.
I'm not especially puffed up.
I dabble in iniquity but don't rejoice in it.
But envy.
Oh envy!
Envy of all that's admirable in everyone,
And not just admirable
But simply nice
Like matched towels in the bathroom.
What I wouldn't give for charity enough
To envy not.

Notebooks

If you could read the notebooks of my life,
(And there are lots), you wouldn't marvel much.
I might improve them with a pleasing style,
But lack, I know, the literary touch.

If you could see the notebooks of my life,
(And there are lots) you'd notice right away
That color, size and subject can be changed
While one surprising feature seems to stay.

Within the notebooks of a lengthy life,
A hidden text is evident in all.
They hide collections of Italian words
For purposes of study and recall.

In all those many notebooks, you might think
For once Italian would have been forgot,
But even in the pages of "Extended trips"
Vocabulary has an honored spot.

Example:
Segnare. Distinguish
Destrier. Charger
Remare. To row
Asta. Spear
Uragano. Hurricane
Monteggiare. Moralize

I often ponder on these random lists,
Asking what metaphors come into play.
Are these the emblems of a life well spent
Or have I frittered half my life away?

To feed a passion forty years or more
Takes dedication and a steadfast will,
A perseverance of unusual force
And deep devotion to linguistic skill.

But then again, what good is listing words
Unused and unremembered in some book
Where they will quickly fade away for good
Without a moment of a second look.

I can't confront these questions any more.
For good or ill, I'm filling up my notebooks as before.

Train Thoughts 1

A sunny beach, a couple and a child,
Glimpsed from my air-conditioned Amtrak train
Have left me curiously stirred
By jealous longings I cannot explain.
I chose this train, this destination and this time.
What great regret has turned my thoughts so wild
That I should wish to vanish from my seat
To be that sunny beach, that couple and that child?

Train Thoughts 2

A sunny beach, my wife, our little son,
Chasing the gulls, but keeping us in sight,
Then rushing back to show us shell or stone.
When did I lose that instinct of delight?
I love these Sunday walks, but when the train goes by,
I fantasize it's going to the moon,
And so am I.

Nobody Wants to Be a Pill

Nobody wants to be a pill.
If wishing would do it, we'd all be charming,
Bursting with energy, bright and disarming,
Easy of humor and ready of will.
Nobody wants to be a pill.

Nobody wants to be a bitch.
If switching could do it, we'd not be demanding,
But sensitive, patient and all understanding,
Our instincts intact and our sympathies rich.
Nobody wants to be a bitch.

Nobody chooses mortality,
But losing our lives is as ancient as sinning,
Try as we may to keep living and winning,
Giving the lie to humanity.
Nobody chooses mortality.

The Bacchae,
Harvard Stadium 1983

Bewitched by Bromius, our senses fail.
We see, we hear, we touch to no avail.
Agave saw a lion, plain as plain,
Could hear him roaring, feel his furry main.
While we, befuddled by the God as much or more
Perceived Kathairon and the palace door.
But poor Agave, when her fit was done,
Beheld no lion but a murdered son,
While we, more lucky, when our spell gave way
Awoke to Cambridge and to glorious May.

Restless Night

Come childhood comforters of waking nights
Come rain, wind, and shining moon
Who used to bless me in my restless bed
And let me sleep.

If now my moon is just a neighbor's window,
My wind, the passing local train,
The rain the furnace, I won't complain.

Watercolor

The purple spot dropped, by mistake
Upon a painted sky will never go away,
Blot as you may.
Attempt to alter it to cloud or bird,
It will not disappear
No more than will a word
You wish you could unsay.
A purple spot's a spot.
And it will stay.

Venezia

Venezia.
A noble name
But still not name enough
For such a place
Where likely words
Fall flat and die
From sheer irrelevance
To wading palaces,
Gondola'd canals
And boats, boats, boats.

At the Campo della Pescaria, see the fish
Massed in splendor on their icy beds.
Heart arresting hoard of fins, shapes, scales and eyes.
Tuna, mackerel, silvery sardines,
Scallops, octopi and eels,
Each with its own perfection,
A Grand Canal of color and of form.

Wordless market,
Wordless city,
Each the offspring of a common sea.
Venezia.

Armor

I bind unto myself this day
The sudden rise of the loon's strange song,
The shining greens against the spruce,
The tiller's feel when the wind goes strong.
I hoard each moment of pure delight
And store it down in my deepest core,
Where the resident demons rant and roar
And stab and trample and bite and shove
And suck the life from the things I love.

I bind unto myself this day
Whatever armor the gods will give,
Be it greens or loons or some other joy
To foil the demons and let me live.
For my deepest core is the demon's lair,
And my only hope is to face them there,
Armed with my weapons of pure delight
And beat them back to their joyless night.

The Cricket Grannies

The tiny cricket grannies
Stretch their raspy legs along their mats.
Illusionless, they still believe in exercise.
They revel in absurdity
And tell each other insect jokes.
Of course they don't forget what once they were,
But that was in another life.
What they do now is rub their raspy legs together
To swell the chorus of the cricket song.

FOR FUN

A Fishing Trip,
Invitation and Reply

The invitation:
Would you like to go with me to where the fishing's
   very bad,
Where the fish are very tiny, (if they're any to be had)
Where the black flies and mosquitoes are much bigger
   than the fish,
And the room to swing a fly rod 's more constricted
   than you'd wish,
And to get there, you must navigate a mile of muddy slush
And half a mile of briars and impenetrable brush?

The reply;
What a splendid proposition for a most delightful day.
When I've packed our luncheon hamper,
   let's depart without delay.

"You've got to Break Eggs
to Make an Omelet"

When people make an awful mess
For some improvement's sake,
They always talk of omelets
And of eggs you have to break.
They ought to leave those eggs alone,
If that's their sole excuse,
I'd give up omelets any day
To end that egg abuse.

Stories Retold

When someone tells a story
Which I've heard and heard and heard,
I want to shout, and sometimes do,
"Don't say another word!"

But if I should repeat myself,
It's always very apt,
So why am I not greeted with
Attention that is rapt?

Poetry Reading

One by one, we rise to the mike to read our poems:
Blank verse,
Rhymed,
Long,
Short,
Good,
Bad,
But greeted all alike with sparse applause
Provided by a smattering of relatives and friends.
Then we sit down,
And feel a satisfaction too profound for understanding
Even by ourselves.

Acknowledgments

I owe boundless gratitude to Domini Dragoone and Lucy Bell Jarka-Sellers without whom this book would never have come to life.

About the Author

Lucy Bell Newlin Sellers was born in Philadelphia in 1935. Having graduated from Radcliffe College, she taught drama first at the Kangaru School in Embu, Kenya, then at the Germantown Friends School in Philadelphia, and finally at the College of the Atlantic in Bar Harbor, Maine, where she directed plays every fall for twenty-three years. During all that time, and afterwards, she was producing a body of poetry. She raised four children with her beloved husband, Peter H. Sellers, and now enjoys grandchildren and great-grandchildren. She splits her time between Philadelphia and Mount Desert Island, Maine.